A Visit to
CHINA

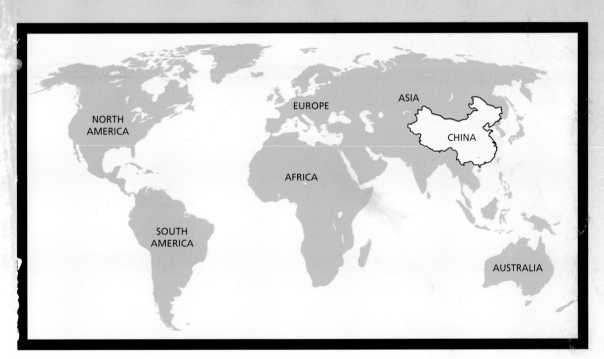

Peter & Connie Roop

Heinemann
LIBRARY

First published in Great Britain by Heinemann Library
Halley Court, Jordan Hill, Oxford OX2 8EJ
a division of Reed Educational and Professional Publishing Ltd.
Heinemann is a registered trademark of Reed Educational & Professional Publishing Limited.

OXFORD FLORENCE PRAGUE MADRID ATHENS
MELBOURNE AUCKLAND KUALA LUMPUR SINGAPORE TOKYO
IBADAN NAIROBI KAMPALA JOHANNESBURG GABORONE
PORTSMOUTH NH CHICAGO MEXICO CITY SAO PAULO

Designed by AMR
Illustrations by Art Construction
Colour Reproduction by Dot Gradations, U.K.
Printed in Hong Kong by Wing King Tong Co., Ltd.

02 01 00 99
10 9 8 7 6 5 4 3 2 1

ISBN 0 431 08320 7
This title is also available in a hardback library edition (ISBN 0 431 018311 8)

Roop, Peter
  A visit to China
  1. China – Social conditions – 1976 – – Juvenile literature
  2. China – Geography – Juvenile literature
  3. China – Social life and customs – 1976 – – Juvenile literature
  I.Title II.China
  951'.059

Acknowledgements

The Publishers would like to thank the following for permission to reproduce photographs:
Heather Angel: pp 16, 18, 19, 24; Biofotos: G&P Corrigan p27; J Allan Cash Ltd: pp 6, 10;
Hutchison Library: pp 13, p22, S Errington p11, F Greene p17, M Macintyre p20, T Page pp 8, 26;
Trip: J Arnold p5, J Batten p7, K Cardwell p12, F Good pp 14, 23, 28, A Tovy p9, B Vikander p15,
M Watson p25; ZEFA: pp 21, 29

Cover photograph reproduced with permission of J Gobert / Robert Harding Picture Library.

Our thanks to Rob Alcraft for his comments in the preparation of this book.

Every effort has been made to contact holders of any material reproduced in this book.
Any omissions will be rectified in subsequent printings if notice is given to the Publisher.

Any words appearing in bold, **like this**, are explained in the Glossary.

Contents

China

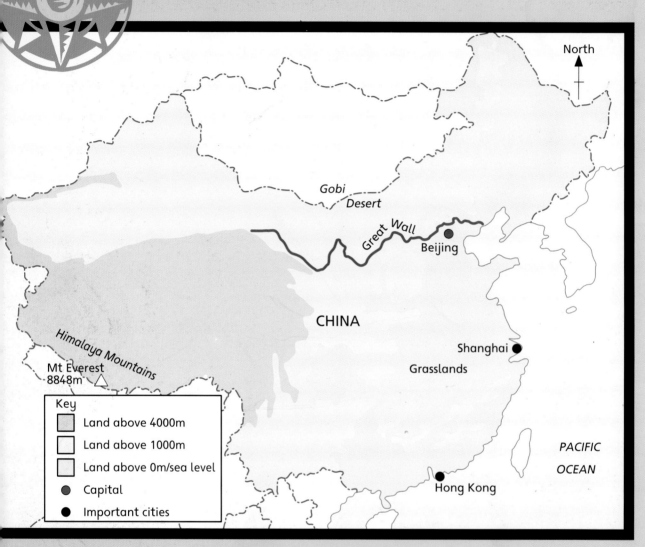

North

Gobi
Desert

Great Wall

Beijing

CHINA

Himalaya Mountains

Mt Everest
8848m

Shanghai

Grasslands

PACIFIC
OCEAN

Hong Kong

Key
- Land above 4000m
- Land above 1000m
- Land above 0m/sea level
- ● Capital
- ● Important cities

More people live in China than in any
other country. The Chinese make up
one-fifth of all the people in the world.

China is in Asia. It is the third largest country in the world. The Chinese call their home The Middle Kingdom.

Land

China **slopes** down from the Himalaya mountains to the Pacific Ocean. In the west, the mountains rise to the **peak** of Mount Everest, the highest mountain on earth.

The middle of China is covered with **grasslands** and **deserts**. The Gobi Desert is here. Most people live in the east, where the green lowlands slope down to the sea.

Landmarks

The Great Wall of China stretches for 6314 km. It would take you a week to drive from one end to the other! The Wall was built long ago to keep out China's enemies.

Shanghai is the largest city in China, but Beijing is the **capital**. Many people go to Beijing to see the Forbidden City. It used to be the palace for the **emperor**.

Homes

Most city homes and flats are small.
They have two or three rooms.
Families share bathrooms and kitchens
with neighbours.

Most Chinese live in the country where homes are larger. Often grandparents, parents and children share the same house.

Food

Most meals are rice or noodles, with
small pieces of meat or vegetables.
A favourite Chinese food is **dumplings**.
People eat with **chopsticks** or spoons.

China also has tea houses. There you can drink tea and eat lots of sweet, sticky cakes. They do not put milk in their tea.

Clothes

In the cities, most Chinese people wear clothes like yours. In the country, people wear loose, baggy clothes. They need to be comfortable while they work in the fields.

On special occasions, many Chinese people dress up. They wear the colourful clothes of their **region**.

Work

Most Chinese people are farmers. They grow rice, tea, wheat or vegetables. Some people also farm chickens, pigs, ducks or fish.

Chinese workers make iron, steel, chemicals, oil and machines. China sells many of these **products** and others, like toys or food, to other countries.

Transport

Most Chinese people travel by foot, bicycle, boat or bus. Cars are very expensive in China. Not many people can **afford** a car.

Trains and lorries carry people and **products** across China. Chinese boats, called junks, sail on rivers and canals. Big ships from around the world visit China's busy **ports**.

language

Most people in China are called Han
Chinese. They speak Mandarin Chinese.

There are also 56 other groups of people in China. These people live, dress and speak differently from the Han Chinese.

School

Children from the age of 6 to 12 go to elementary school. They learn science, maths, Chinese, English, history, geography, art and physical education.

To read well, Chinese children must learn an alphabet of 6000 **symbols**. Each symbol has its own meaning.

Free time

Chinese children play football (soccer), basketball, volleyball, table tennis and chess. They also like making and flying kites. But they spend most time helping at home.

Most Chinese exercise every day. They ride
bikes to work or do kung fu. Older people
exercise by dancing, riding bikes or doing a
stretching exercise called tai chi.

Celebrations

Everyone tries to be at home for the five day Spring Festival. People dress up in their best clothes, visit friends and eat niangao (sticky cake). They also enjoy lion dancing in the **parades**.

National Day celebrates the **founding** of the People's Republic of China. People celebrate with sports, bands, parades and noisy fireworks.

The Arts

China is famous for its pictures of nature on china, paper and silk. Other popular Chinese arts are cutting delicate pictures out of paper and painting **symbols** with a paintbrush.

Chinese people enjoy the **opera**. The clever, kind Monkey King is a favourite opera character. The **audience** shout 'Hao!' when when an actor does an excellent job.

Factfile

Name	The full name of China is the People's Republic of China.
Capital	The **capital** city is Beijing.
Language	Most Chinese people speak Mandarin Chinese.
Population	There are more than 1 billion people living in China.
Money	Instead of the dollar or pound, the Chinese have the yuan.
Religions	Many Chinese people believe in Taoism, Confucianism, Buddhism, Islam or Christianity.
Products	China produces lots of coal, rice, machines, oil, steel and cement.

Words you can learn

ni hao (nee how)	hello
zaijian (zay-GEE-en)	goodbye
xiexie (SHE-a-shay)	thank you
shide (SURE-duh)	yes
bu shi (BOO sure)	no
yi	one
er	two
san	three

Glossary

afford	have enough money to buy or use something
audience	the group of people who watch something
capital	the city where the government is based
chopsticks	a pair of sticks held in one hand to lift food to the mouth
course	stages in a meal, like pudding
desert	a large area of land that has almost no rain and very few plants and animals
dumplings	dough mixture with meats and vegetables inside, which is cooked in boiling water or steam
emperor	the person like a king, who ruled China a long time ago
grasslands	large, flat areas of land where grasses are the only plants which grow
founding	when something like a country is started
opera	a play with music and singing
parades	a group of people on show, dancing or walking together
peak	the top of a mountain
ports	the places where ships pick up and drop off the goods they are carrying
products	things which are grown, taken from the earth, made by hand or made in a factory
region	an area or part of a country
slopes	where the land goes from high up to lower down
symbol	a shape or sign that has a special meaning

Index